ARCHETYPES

a Catalogue

by Alastair Fontana

ARTSEDIMENTS PUBLISHING

First published by Artsediments Group in 2012
Published by Artsediments Group in 2014
1 2
Copyright © Alastair Fontana 2012
The moral right of the author has been asserted.

All translations are by the author.

ISBN: 1496042948
ISBN-13: 978-1496042941

Archetypes were believed to be pure entities. They were the immortal Gods epitomizing the basic forces of nature, such as Venus for love or Mars for war. A human being was considered just an imperfect mixture of the divine archetypes.

However, I think differently. The way I see it, archetypes are complex rather than pure forms. They are not divine, but human. I imagine them as rare and intricate individuals. Unique beings leaving an indelible impression on our souls like Achilles and Ulysses, the mortal heroes who inspired the greatest poems of all time.

During the years I lived in Italy, I took pictures of the archetypes I knew there, dear and peculiar friends I had the good fortune to meet. The use of the camera in these photographs was intentionally dry. The subjects were not permitted to pose for the picture, and I did not try to compose the images in any way. No room for embellishments was allowed.

When years later I found back these pictures, I was surprised by the strength they emanated, by the heroic stature of the subjects, and by their timeless nature. Combined with fragments of The Iliad and The Odyssey, the silent images started speaking with the voices of Hector, Helen, and Achilles. This is how this book, a personal tribute to friendship and humanity, came to existence.

Alastair Fontana

"And then there is the sweetness of love,
The languid heat of desire
Capable of driving the wisest man insane."

Homer, The Iliad, book XIV

Roberta
(Chef)

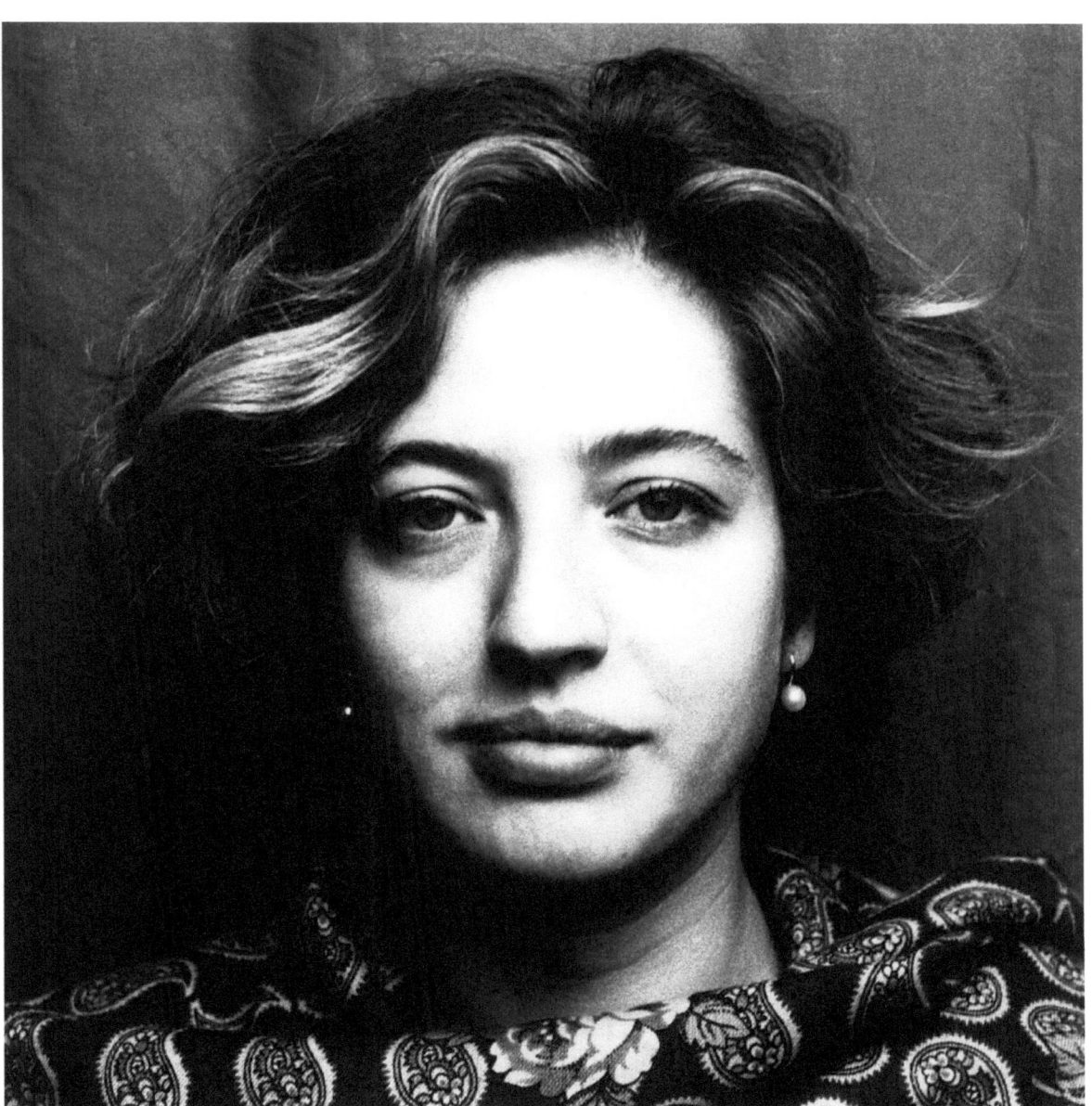

"He came down
Like nightfall."

Homer, The Iliad, book I

Alfredo
(Lawyer)

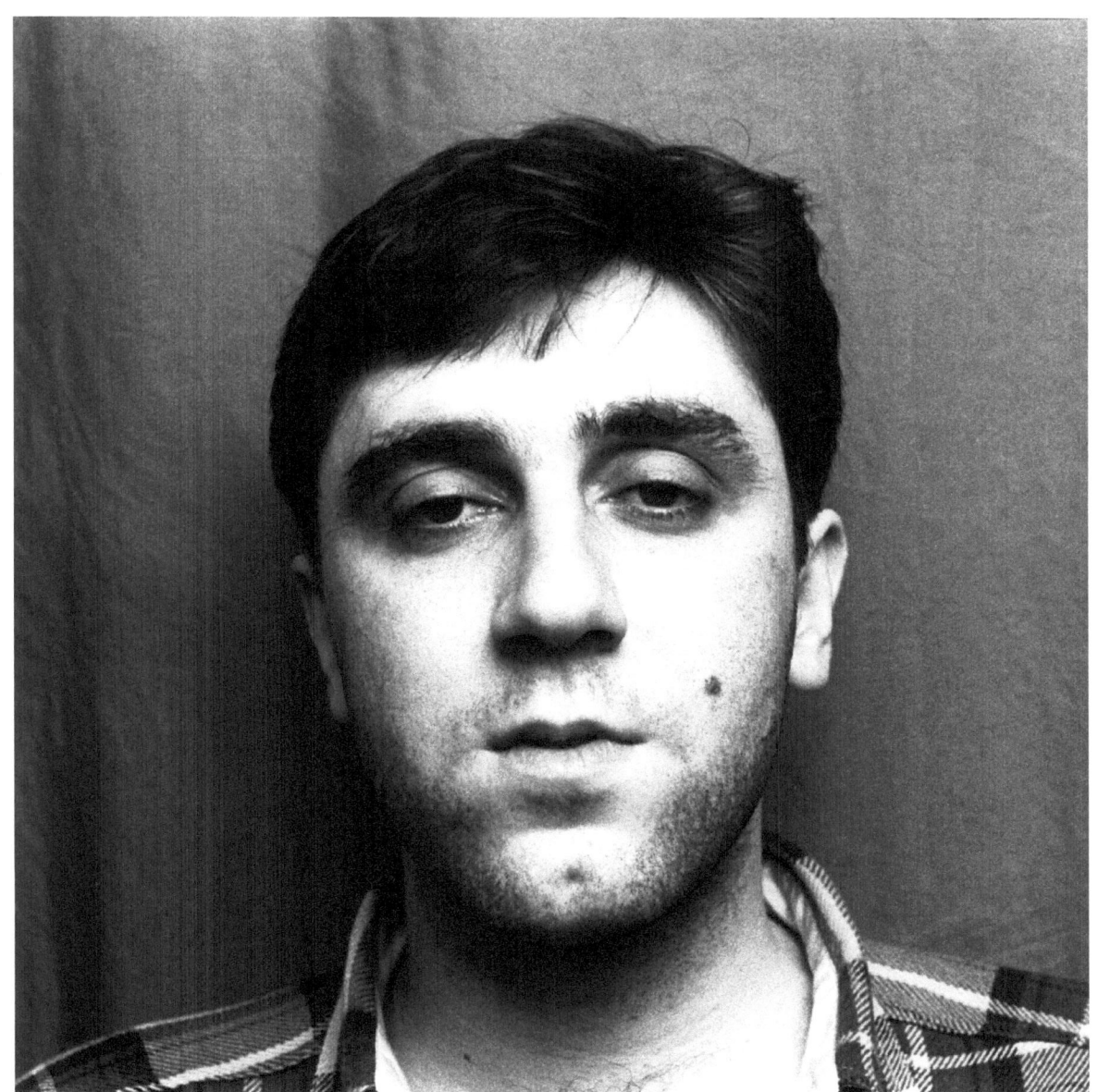

"A roaring sea lies between us,
And many somber mountains."

Homer, The Iliad, book I

Gino
(Biologist)

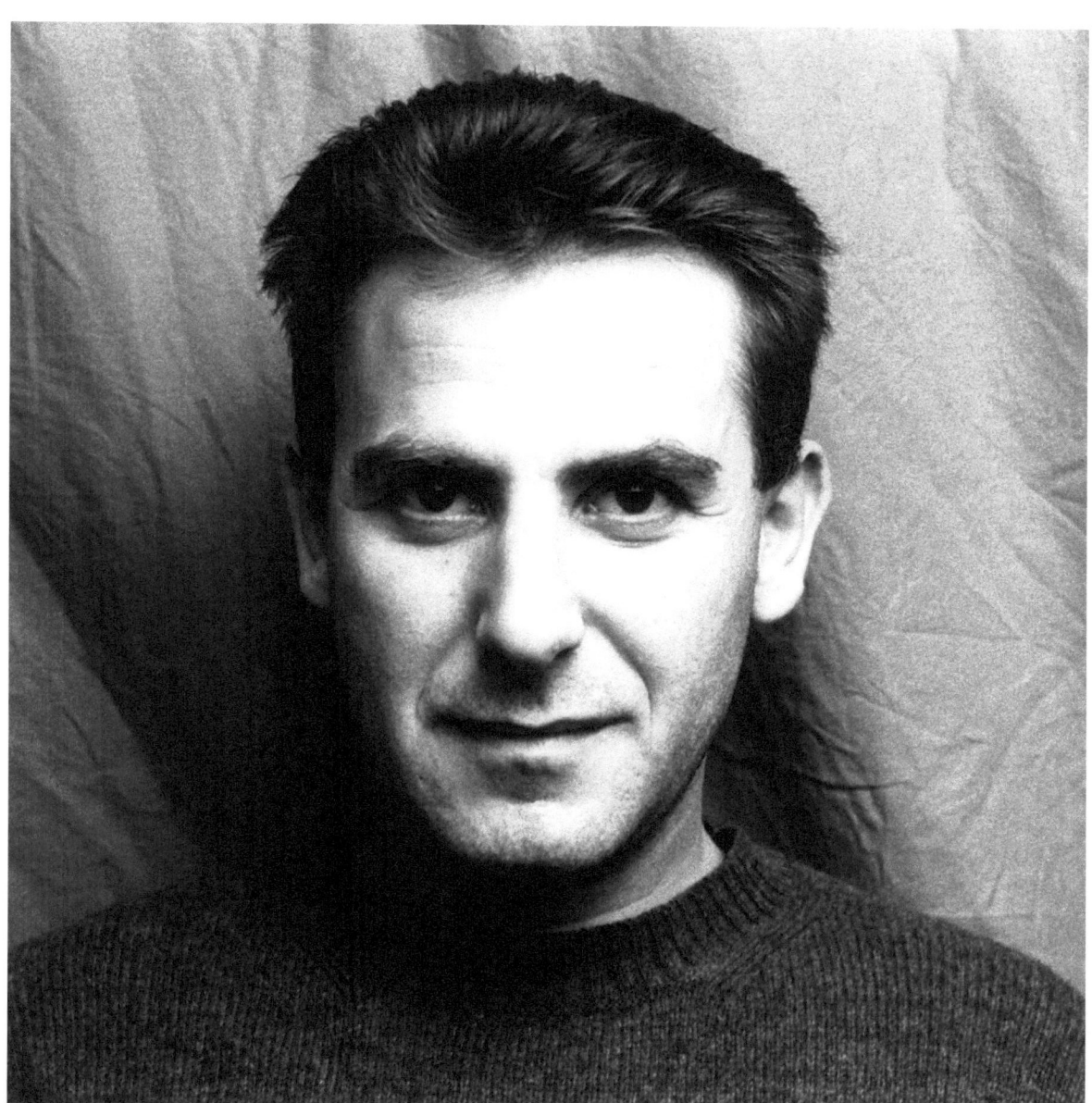

"A deathless goddess
Of unbearable beauty,
So terrifyingly and divinely lovely."

Homer, The Iliad, book III

Daniela

(Actress)

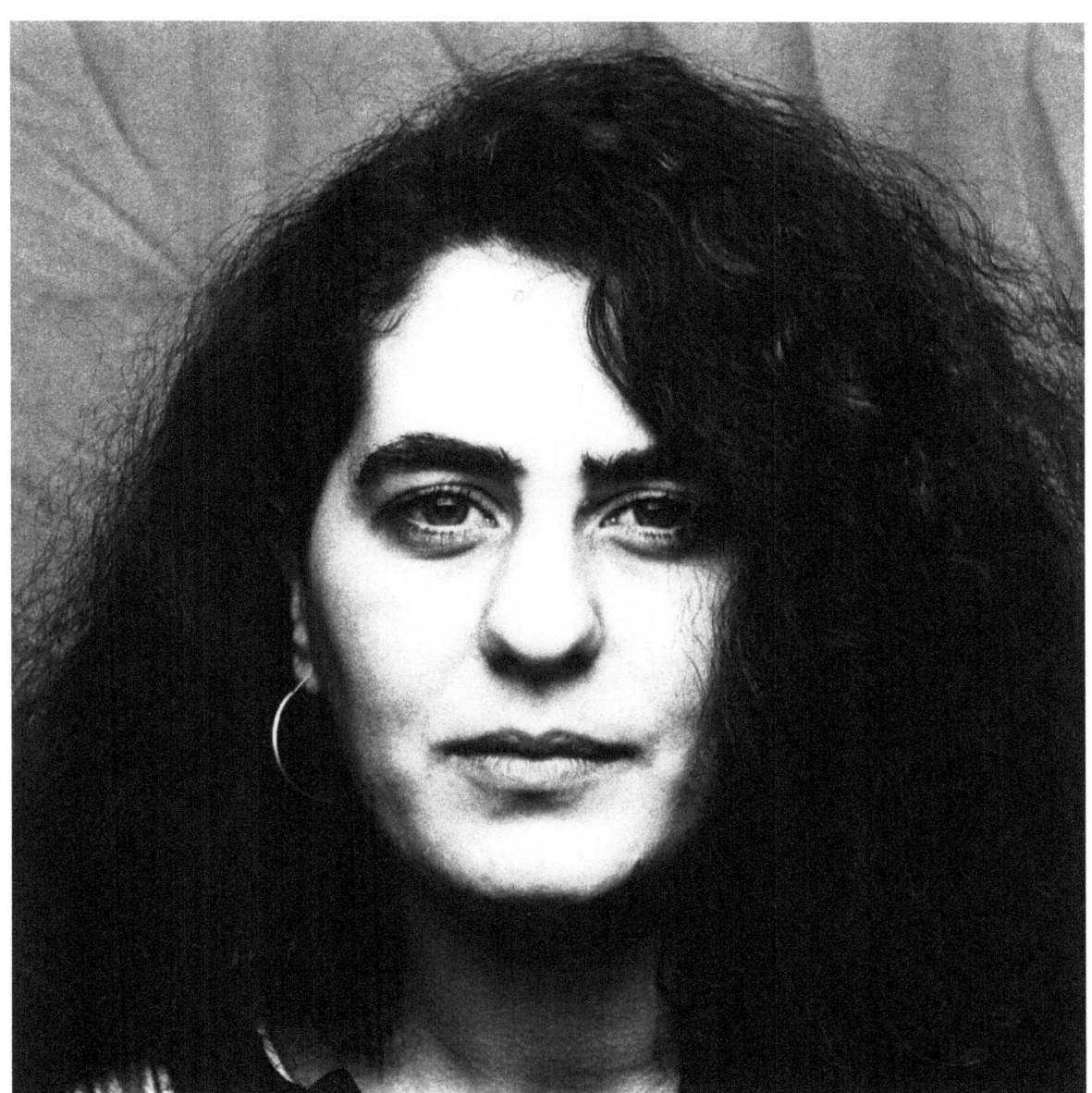

"Push on, ye horse-taming Trojans,
Break through the wall of the Greeks,
And hurl among the ships
a fiercely blazing fire."

Homer, The Iliad, book XII

Mario

(Horse trainer)

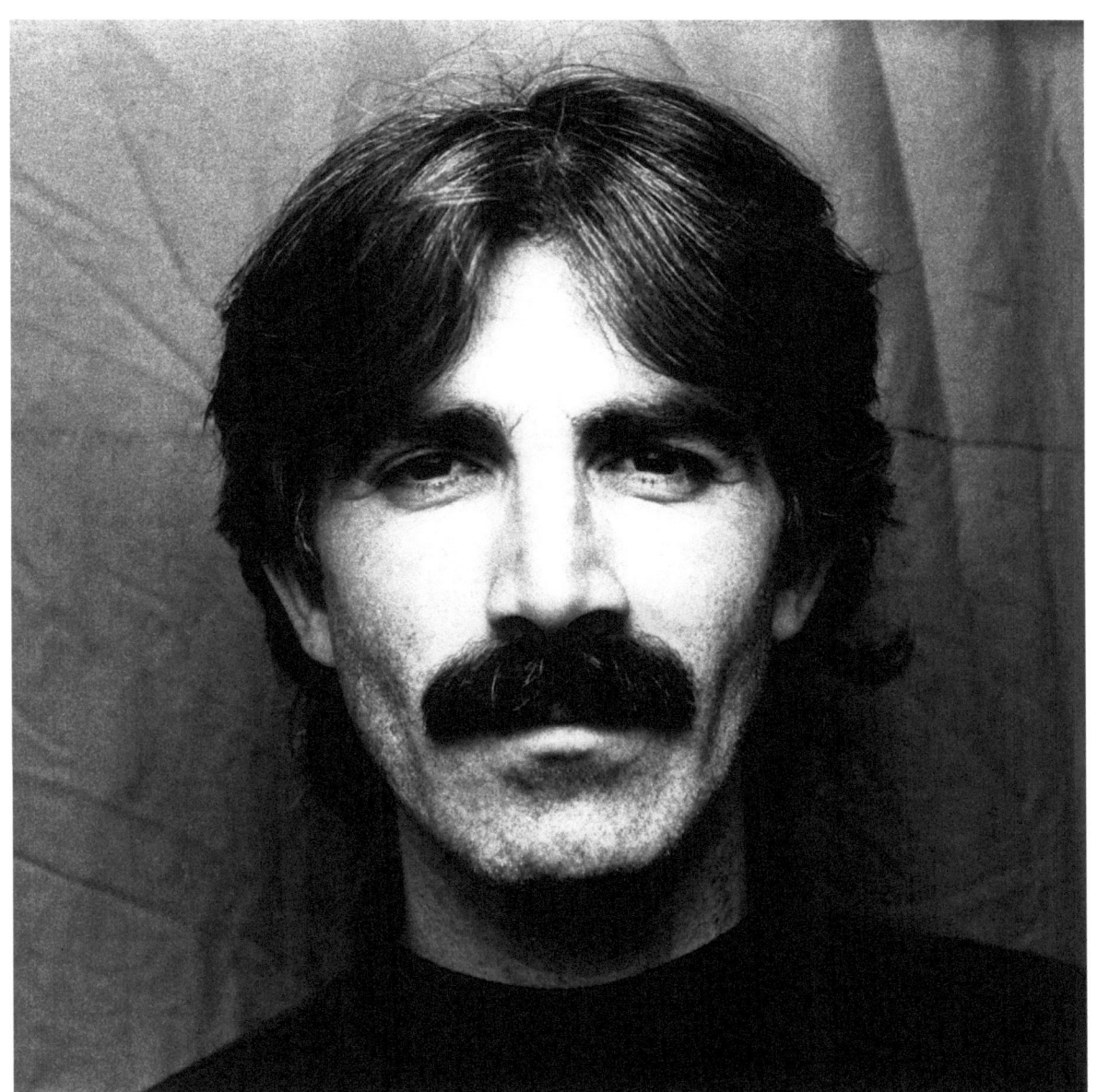

"We're doomed
And yet we will live forever,
For generation of men to come,
In songs."

Homer, The Iliad, book VI

Nico
(Musician)

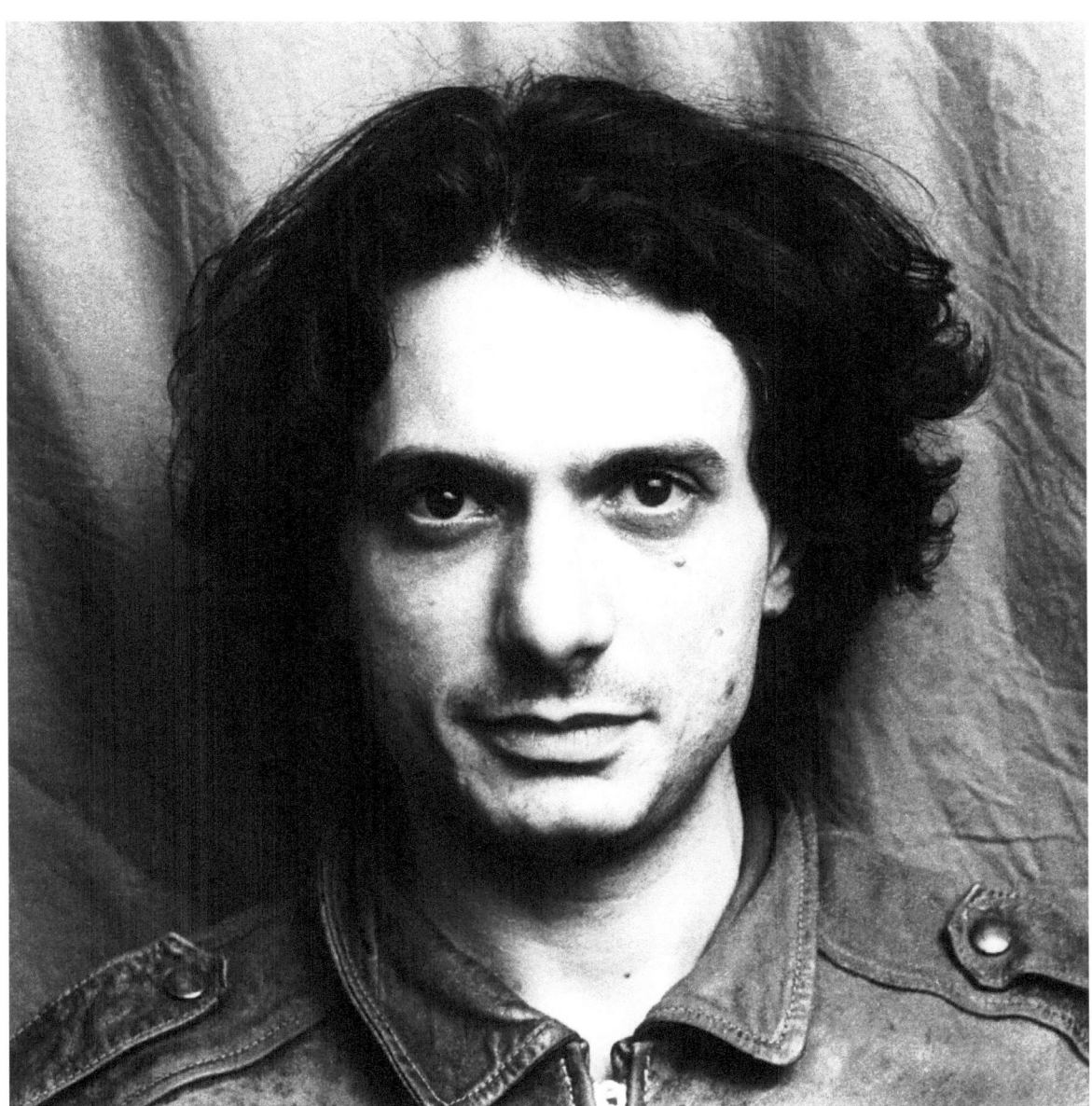

"Was it all just a dream?"

Homer, The Iliad, book III

Oriana

(Dancer)

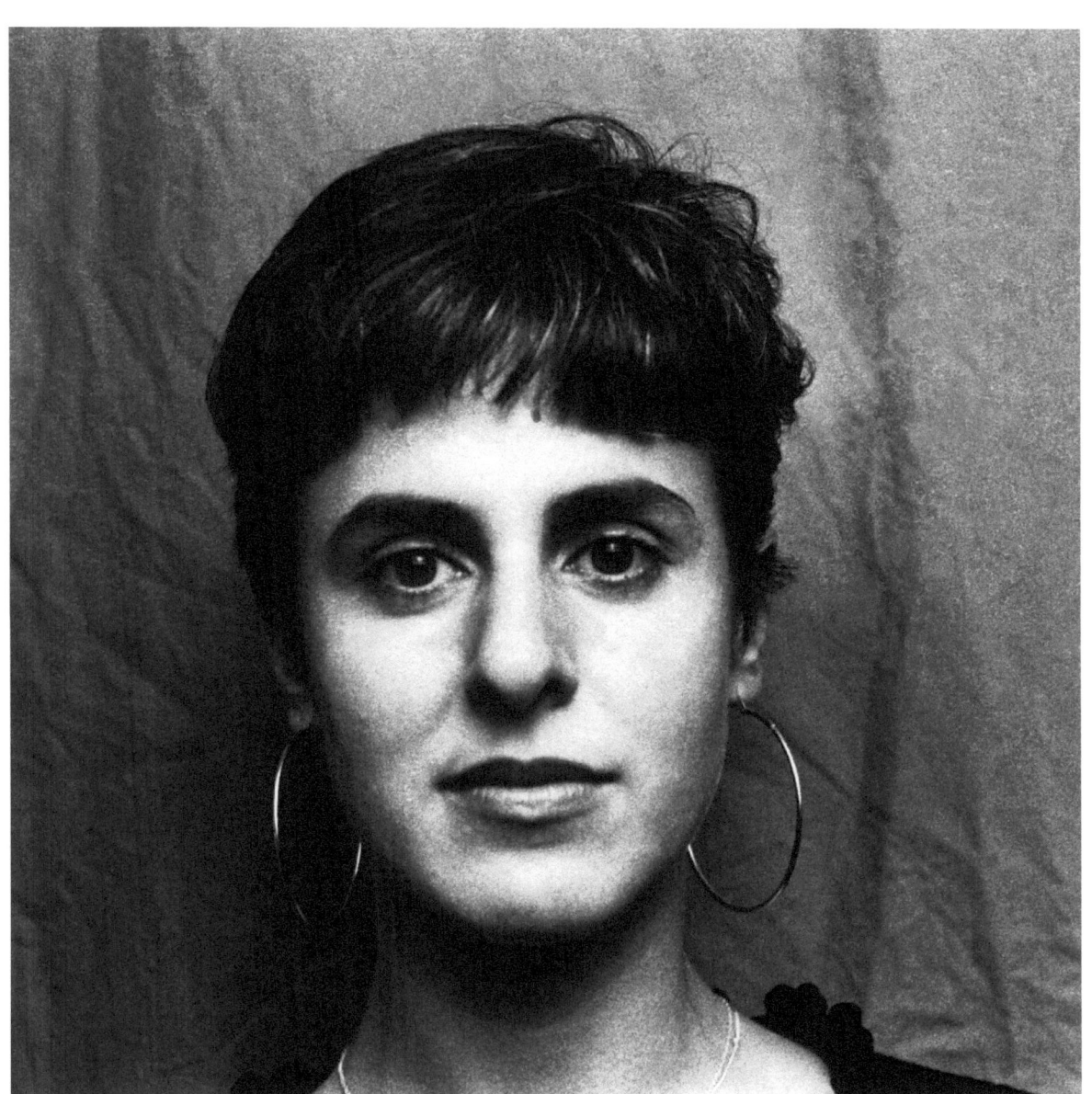

"Be always the best,
And stand out above the rest."

Homer, The Iliad, book VI

Matteo
(Psychiatrist)

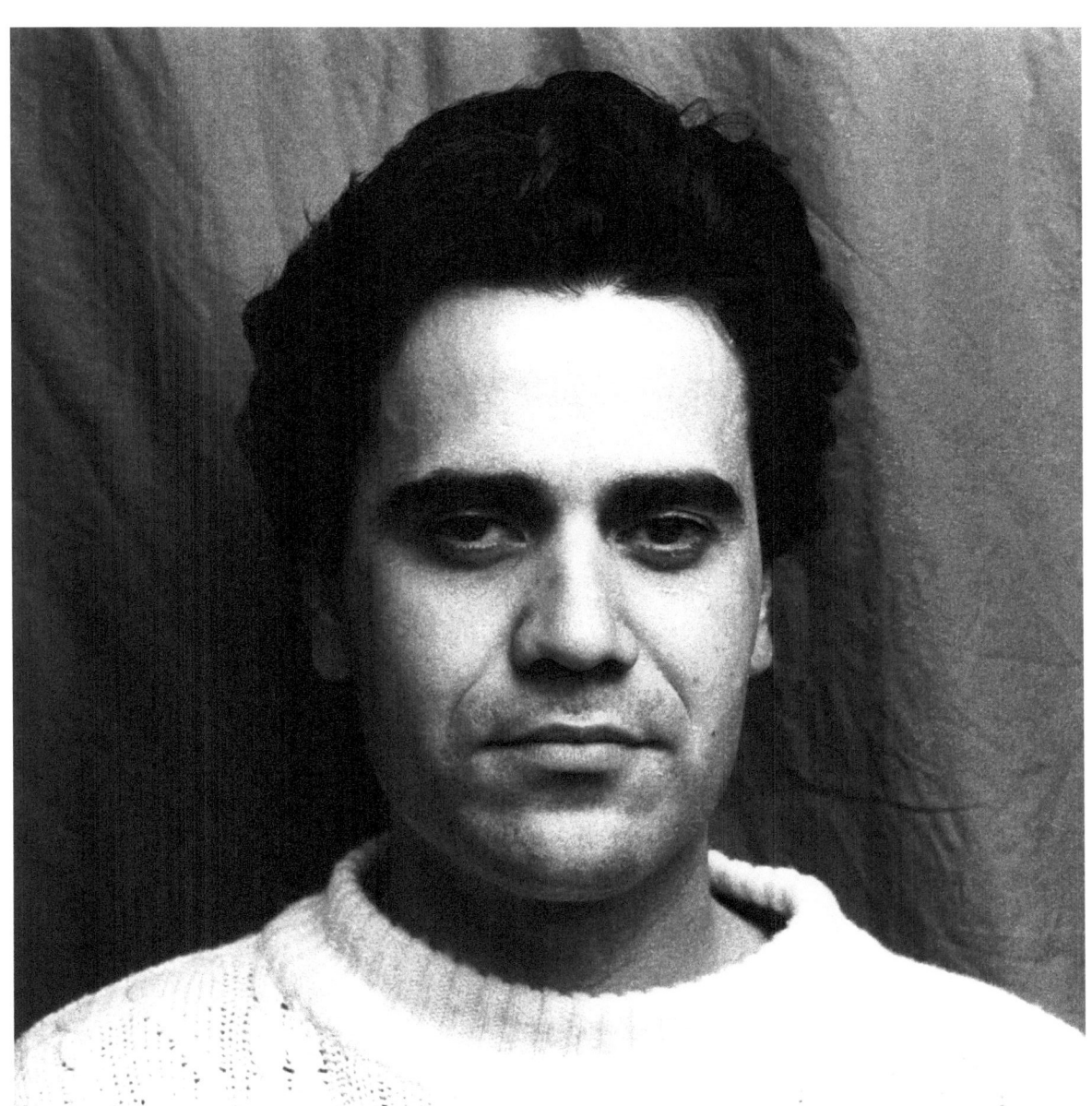

"Antilochus!
You're the worst driver
In the whole world!
Go to hell!"

Homer, The Iliad, book XXIII

Cippo
(Motorcyclist)

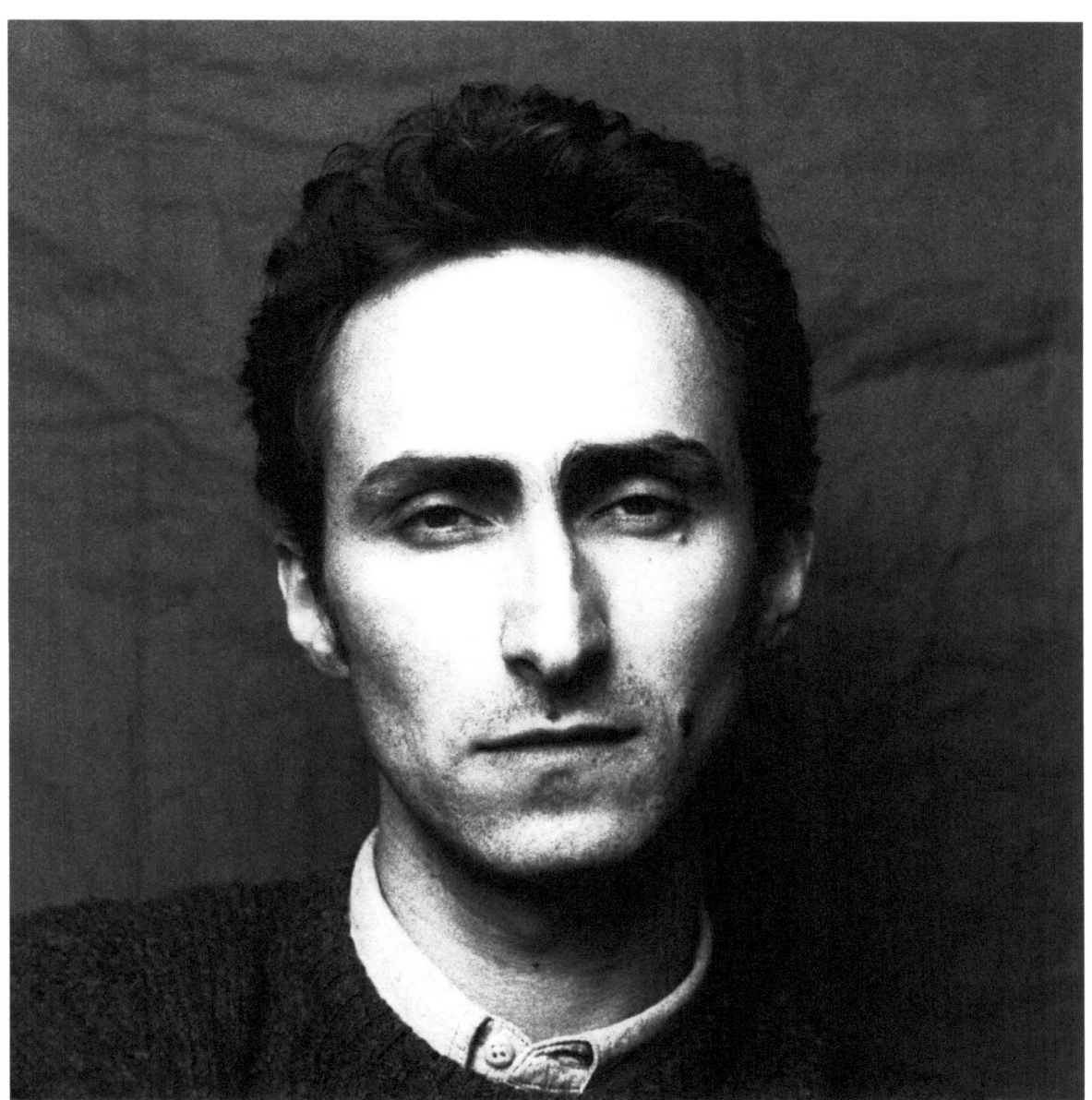

> "And she smiled,
> Smiled through her tears."
>
> *Homer, The Iliad, book VI*

Lidia
(Screenwriter)

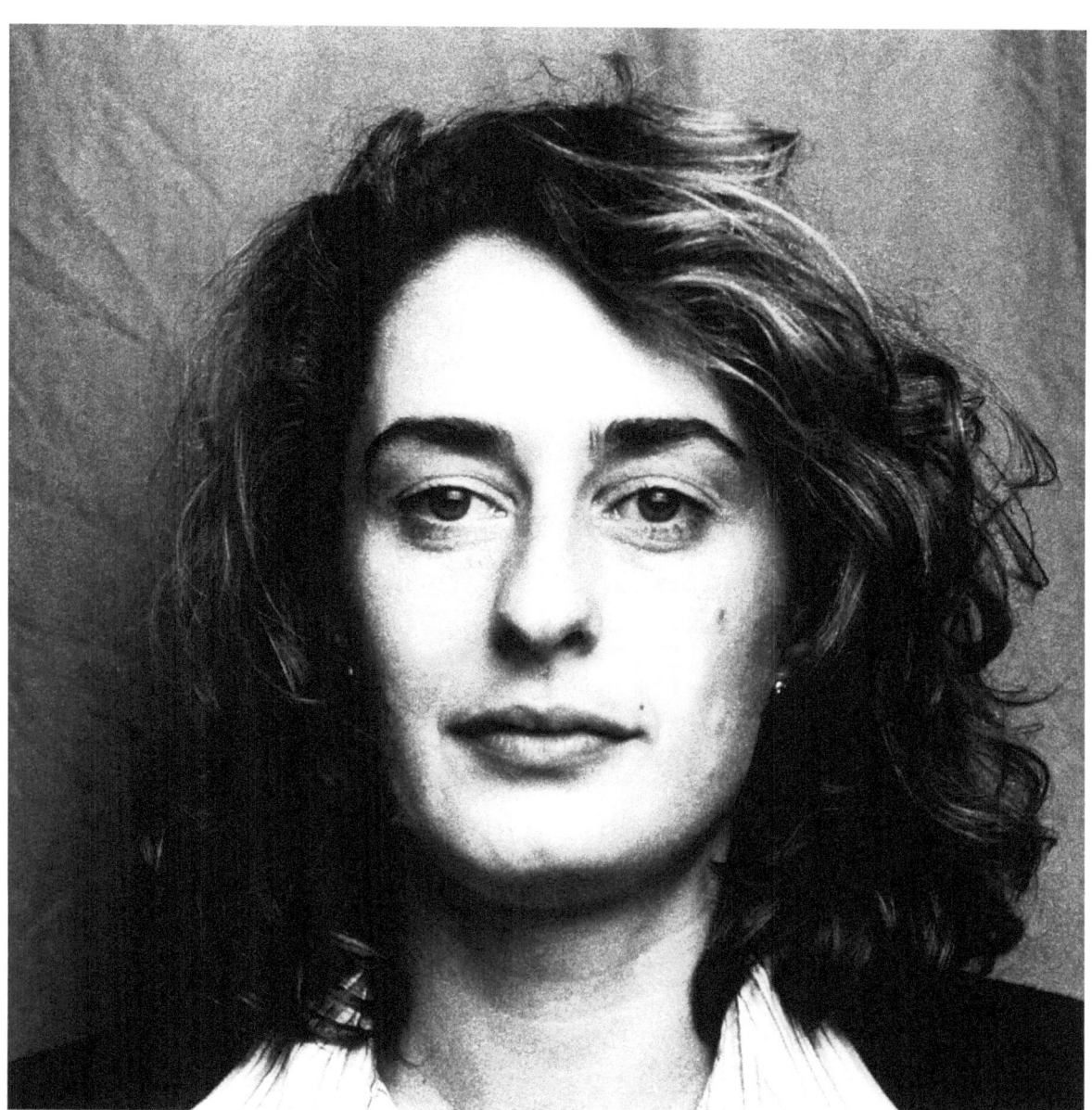

"Enough!
Bygones shall be bygones now.
What is done is done."

Homer, The Iliad, book XVIII

Lello

(Geologist)

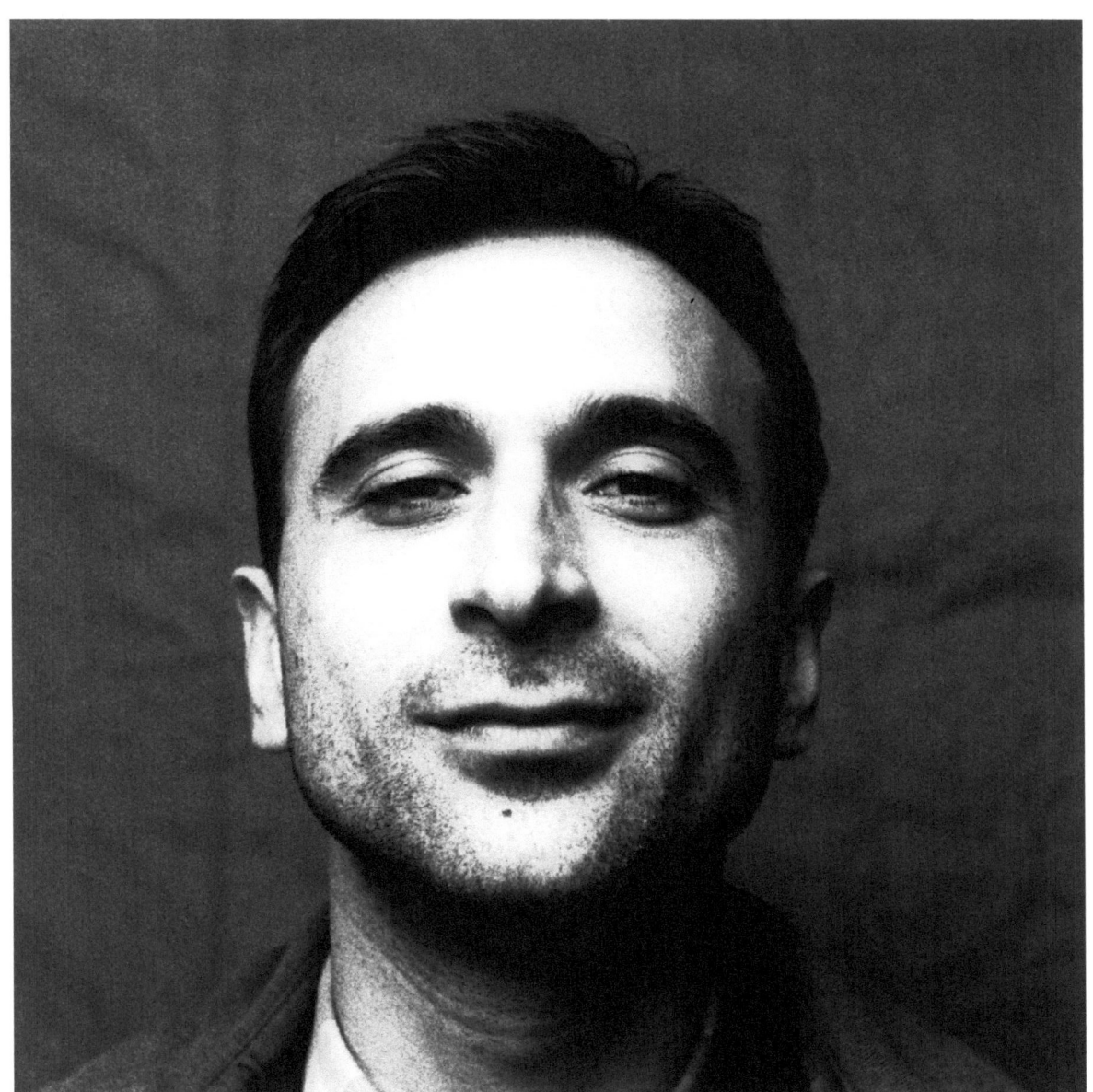

"There is a time for speech,
And there is also a time for sleep."

Homer, The Odyssey, book XI

Michele

(Film director)

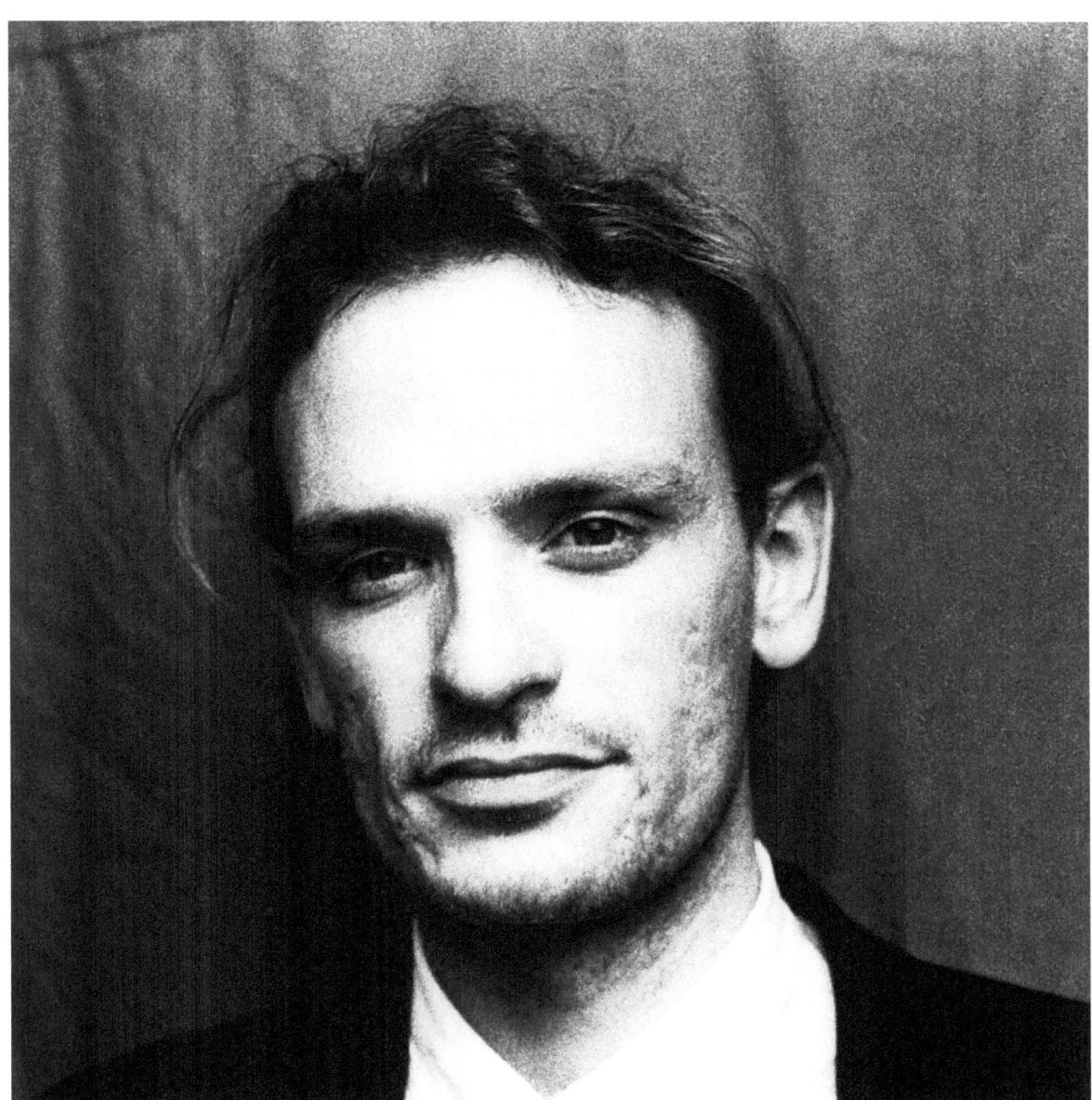

"A small rock
A Dashing wave
Can tame."

Homer, The Odyssey, book III

Enrichetta

(Scholar)

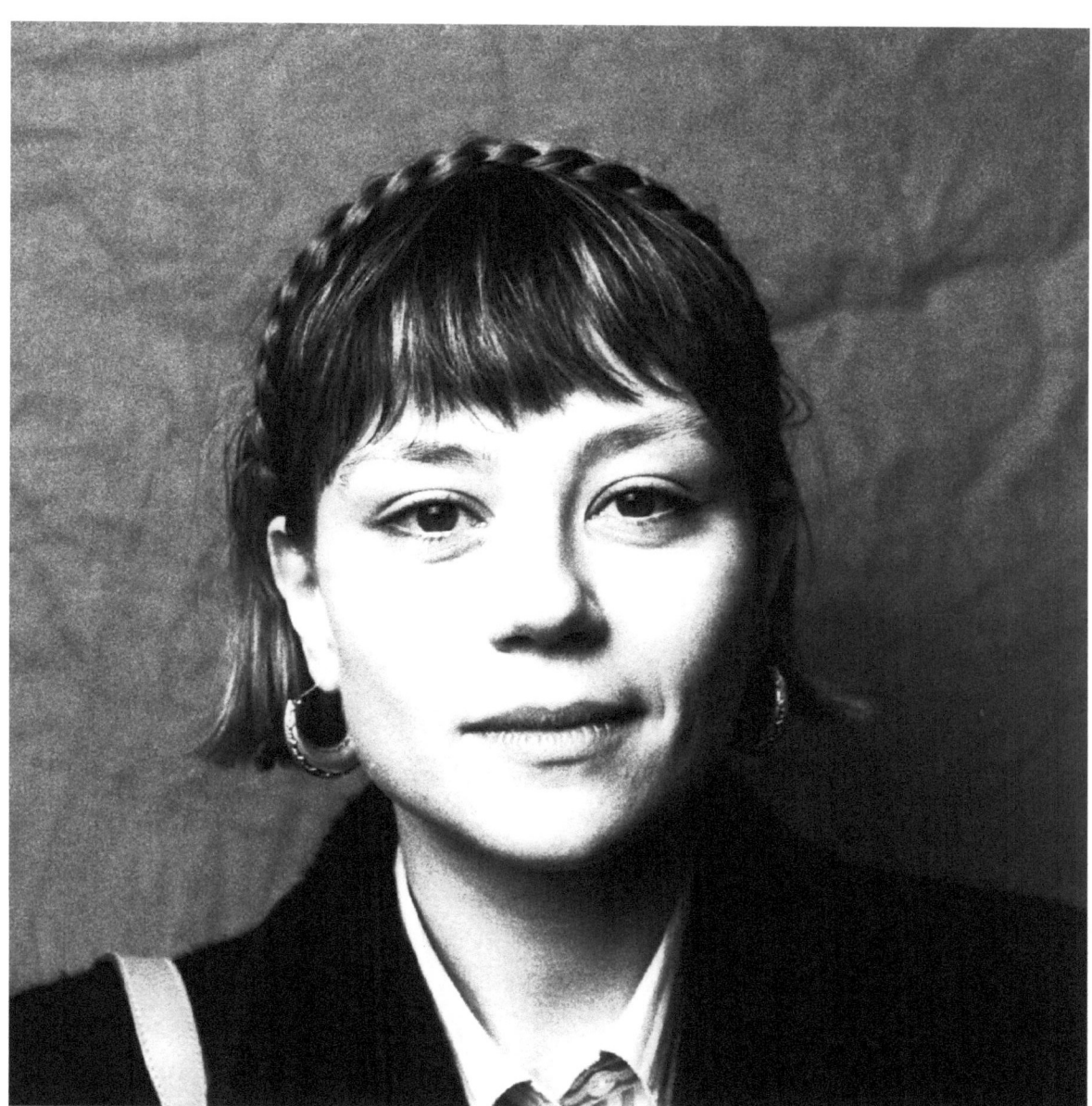

"A friend with an understanding heart
Is dear to me like a brother."

Homer, The Odyssey, book VIII

Francesco

(Saxophonist)

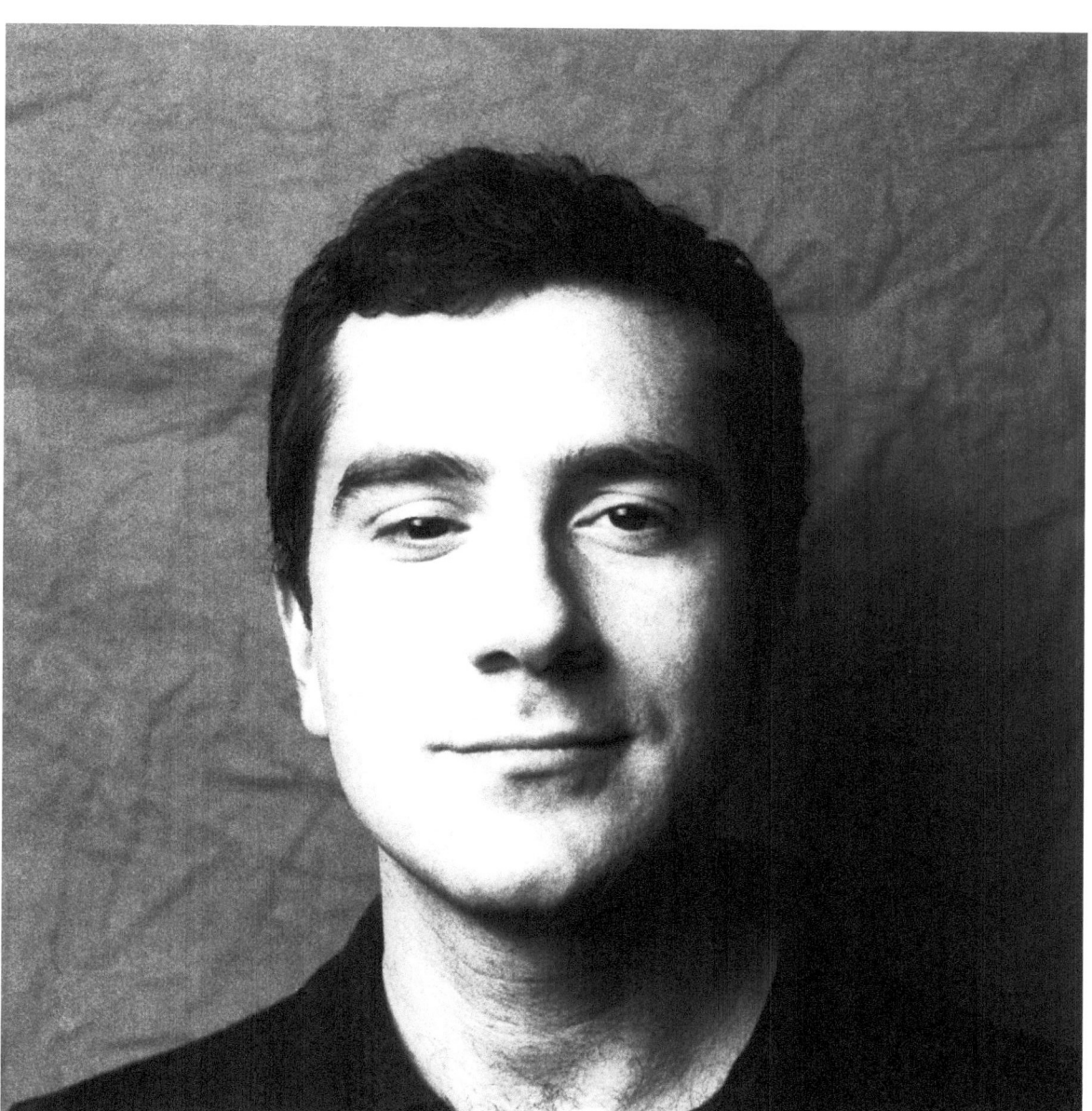

"How vain,
Without the merit,
Is the fame."

Homer, The Iliad, book XVII

Gianfranco

(Physicist)

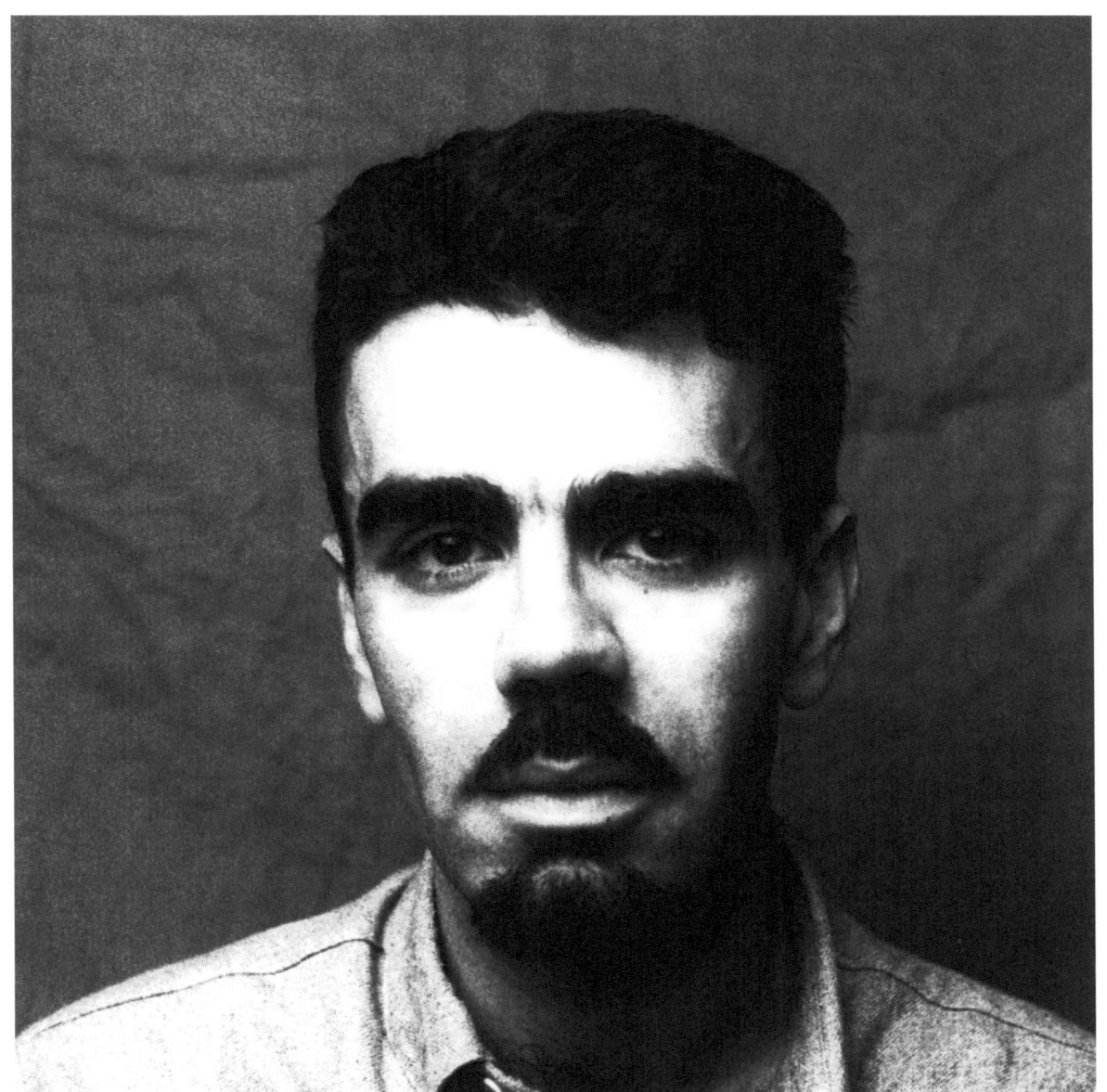

"Like that star of the fading summer
Rising brighter than all others
After bathing in the ocean stream."

Homer, The Iliad, book V

Cinzia
(Astronomer)

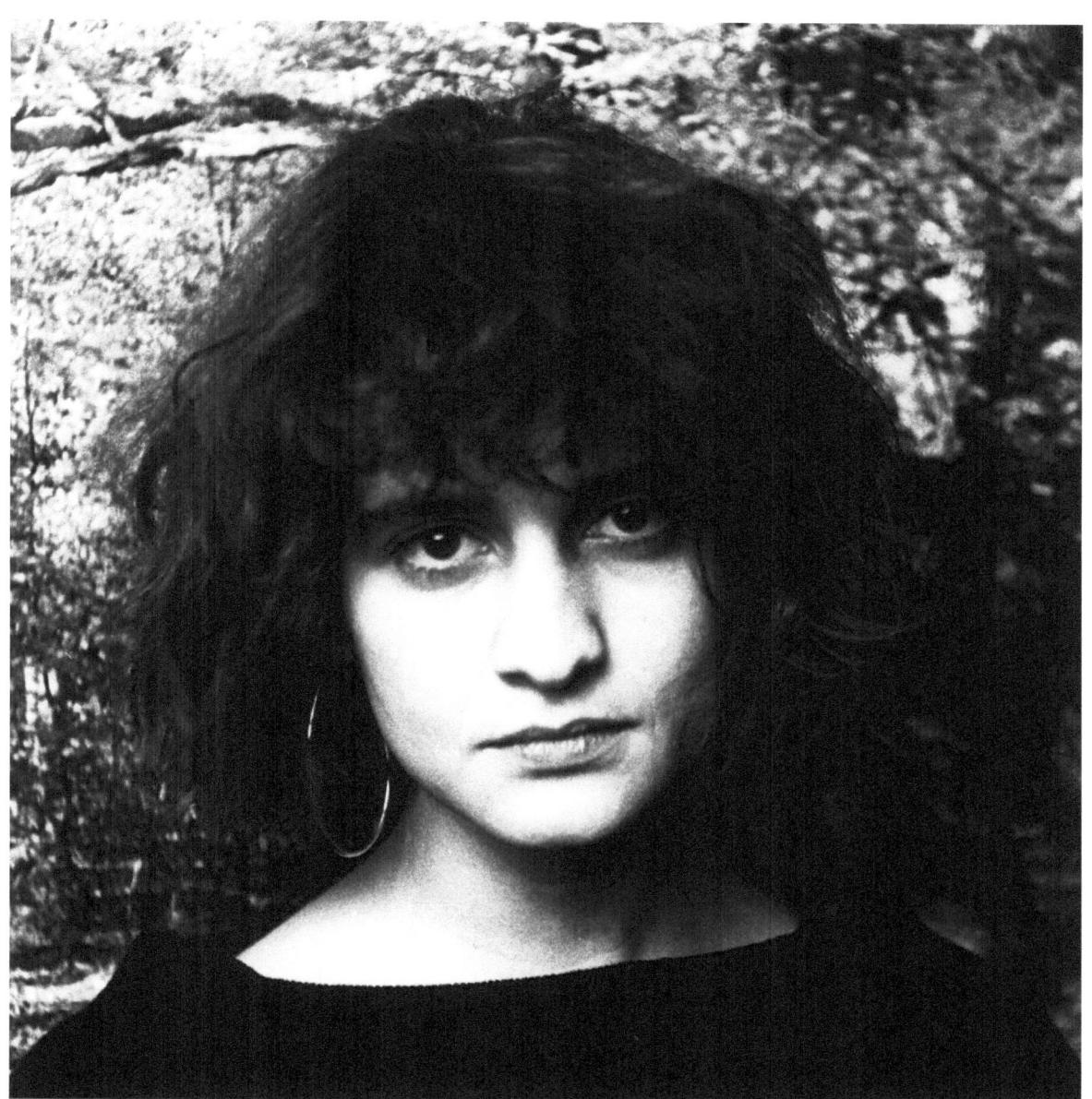

About the Author

Alastair Fontana spent most of his life between Europe and America. He was educated in Italy and has lived in such diverse places as Madison, Lausanne, Brussels, and San Francisco, among others. He is articulate in English, Italian and French. He likes traveling and loves writing. Among his interests are visual art, photography, and cooking.

www.ingramcontent.com/pod-product-compliance
Lightning Source LLC
Chambersburg PA
CBHW050402180526
45159CB00005B/2117